FRANK, WHO LIKED TO BUILD

To Ralph
—D.B.

To Marek and Iwona
—M.B.

KAR-BEN PUBLISHING®
An imprint of Lerner Publishing Group, Inc.
241 First Avenue North
Minneapolis, MN 55401 USA

Website address: www.karben.com

Photo credits: AP Photo/Nick Ut, p. 30 (left); Pres Panayotov/Shutterstock.com, p. 30 (top); Rudy Mareel/Shutterstock.com, p. 30 (middle); Chaiwat Areeraksa/Shutterstock.com, p. 30 (bottom); Dino Quinzani/Wikimedia Commons (CC BY-SA 2.0), p. 31 (top); Sam Lund/Independent Picture Service, p. 31 (middle); EMP|SFM/Wikimedia Commons (CC BY-SA 3.0), p. 31 (bottom).

Main body text set in ITC Avant Garde Gothic Std medium.
Typeface provided by Adobe.

Library of Congress Cataloging-in-Publication Data

Names: Blumenthal, Deborah, author. | Brzozowska, Maria, 1992– illustrator.
Title: Frank, who liked to build : the architecture of Frank Gehry / Deborah Blumenthal ; illustrated by Maria Brzozowska.
Description: Minneapolis : Kar-Ben Publishing, [2021] | Audience: Ages 4–9 | Audience: Grades K–1 | Summary: "As a child, Frank Gehry liked to dream and play, eventually becoming an architect who created astounding buildings that attract millions of visitors worldwide" —Provided by publisher.
Identifiers: LCCN 2021016263 (print) | LCCN 2021016264 (ebook) | ISBN 9781541597624 | ISBN 9781541597631 (paperback) | ISBN 9781728444185 (ebook)
Subjects: LCSH: Gehry, Frank O., 1929-—Juvenile literature. | Architects—United States—Biography—Juvenile literature.
Classification: LCC NA737.G44 B57 2021 (print) | LCC NA737.G44 (ebook) | DDC 720.92 [B]—dc23

LC record available at https://lccn.loc.gov/2021016263
LC ebook record available at https://lccn.loc.gov/2021016264

Manufactured in the United States of America
1-47866-48312-5/6/2021

FRANK, WHO LIKED TO BUILD

THE ARCHITECTURE OF FRANK GEHRY

DEBORAH BLUMENTHAL

illustrated by **MARIA BRZOZOWSKA**

KAR-BEN
PUBLISHING

IMAGINE A BUILDING

with sloping silver skin
that seems to shiver
in the wind.

Or another
with billowy blanket walls,
big enough to hide
a family of dinosaurs.

And who made them?

Frank Gehry,
an architect.

Some of his buildings look like he designed them
while dreaming
or standing on his head.
Like a kid
having fun.

One has titanium walls
like unrolled
aluminum foil.

Another has giant glass sails enclosing an iceberg.

Imagine tossing building blocks
into a blender
and pureeing them.
Because Frank was different from other people,
so are his buildings.

They curve and swerve
and undulate

like swimming fish,

flowing with time
and light.

Frank started with ordinary
and shaped it
into
extraordinary.

When he was small,
his grandma, Leah, gave him bits of wood
from a sack for the woodstove
and off he went
creating little cities
and different worlds.

Frank's father wasn't impressed.
"He thought I was a dreamer," Frank said.
"He didn't think I would amount to anything.
Neither did my mother."
Those thoughts haunted him
his whole life.

But dreamers keep dreaming.

And playing.

Frank made rooftops that bend and sway.

Boulders that collide
with drenching colors that
steal your sight,

blinding you with brilliance.

Life sometimes
gets in the way of art, though.
Frank was Jewish, and
Jews faced prejudice
in Canada, where he grew up,
and in Los Angeles, where he went
to architecture school.

So he changed his Jewish name—Goldberg—
to Gehry.

But it pained him
to do it.

What he didn't lose
were the memories . . .

Like the chunks of dough his grandma would
give him to play with when she was baking challah—
that became Frank's homemade clay—
so he could change the shape of things.

And the live fish she bought at the market,
dropped into the bathtub
to stay fresh.

Frank was hypnotized
by their water ballet.

Only when he was older
did he realize
the carp that disappeared
from the tub went into
his gefilte fish.

When he became an architect,
Frank kept those fish alive
in his fish lamps,

in his curving and
swerving jewelry,

and in
giant fish sculptures
with shiny skin.

And maybe the graceful way
the carp swam
and swam,
and his love of sailing and the water
explain the curves in his buildings,
like the Guggenheim Museum in Bilbao, Spain,

the Fondation Louis Vuitton in Paris,

and the IAC office building in New York
with its billowing glass sails.

The buildings are all different,
but they started out the same way:
sketches that look like squiggly scribbles,
done in airports and hotel rooms
whenever Frank had a free moment.

Then came the models.
No fancy materials,
just cardboard or wood,
to study,
play,
and invent with.
Frank changed them again and again,
scratching his head
until he got it right.

But even after the buildings were built,
Frank still had doubts.

The first time he saw
the Guggenheim Museum in Bilbao, Spain,
he thought, "What
have I done to these people?"

Still, he kept working,
using metal
and chain mail fencing,
glass and stone,
turning old into new,
turning life on its head.

He used scraps of whatever was around—
paper towel rolls,
pleated cardboard,
even glass bottles—
studying,
playing,
inventing,
dreaming,
seeing possibilities.

Starting with ordinary
and shaping it into
extraordinary,
one building at a time.

AUTHOR'S NOTE

Frank Gehry's buildings don't look like buildings.

They look like art projects made by someone who got carried away playing with shapes, lines, colors, and a dazzling assortment of materials.

Gehry's architecture stuns. It shocks. It takes your breath away. My reaction to seeing a Gehry design always brings me back to my first look at the Grand Canyon. I fell silent, transported to a higher place.

Olympic Fish Pavilion, Barcelona, Spain

Some of the most respected architects in the world are Gehry's biggest fans. When Philip Johnson first saw Gehry's Guggenheim Museum in Bilbao, Spain, he began to sob. "I get the same feeling in Chartres Cathedral," he said. He called Gehry, "the greatest architect we have today," and the Guggenheim Bilbao, "the greatest building of our time."

Frank Gehry

Guggenheim Museum, Bilbao, Spain

Fondation Louis Vuitton, Paris, France

Dancing House,
Prague, Czech Republic

At The World's Jewish Museum in Tel-Aviv, Gehry talked about how his Jewish identity inspired his work: "When I was a kid my grandfather read Talmud to me and that stuck with me because it started with the word why . . . the curiosity that we've been raised with, all of us from childhood is what makes us produce . . . to make things you have to be curious and wonder why and explore and be willing to take chances and risks, but it is from that basic curiosity that is so eloquently written about in the Talmud."

The works of Frank Gehry, the most famous architect in the world, can be seen all over the globe. Each one is fresh, brash, energetic, fascinating, and unique. They may start out as squiggles and sketches, but the latest digital technology turns them into stone and steel.

Still, what's most important to Gehry isn't what comes out of a computer.

The Frederick R. Weisman Art Museum,
Minneapolis,
Minnesota

A life-size photograph of a Greek statue of a charioteer from 500 BCE is outside Gehry's office. In an interview with *Forbes* magazine in 2015, he said, "That unknown artist did a statue that made me cry. How did he do that? That's our goal, emotion."

In 1989 Frank O. Gehry received the Pritzker Architecture Prize, the Nobel of architecture, given for a lifetime of achievement. But back then, at the age of sixty, he was only getting started.

Museum of
Pop Culture,
Seattle, Washington

SELECTED BIBLIOGRAPHY

There are many resources for more information on Frank Gehry. Two that I found particularly helpful are these:

Goldberger, Paul. *Building Art: The Life and Work of Frank Gehry.* New York: Alfred A. Knopf, 2015.

Pollack, Sydney, Ultan Guilfoyle, Frank O. Gehry, Philip Johnson, Bob Geldof, and Barry Diller. *Sketches of Frank Gehry.* Culver City, CA: Sony Pictures Home Entertainment, 2006.

ABOUT THE AUTHOR

Deborah Blumenthal is an award-winning journalist and the author of twenty-five books for adults and children. She was a regular contributor to the *New York Times*, and her features have appeared in a wide variety of national newspapers and magazines. She lives in New York City.

ABOUT THE ILLUSTRATOR

Maria Brzozowska was born in Poland and spent most of her childhood growing up in Turkey, where she now lives. A graduate of Leeds Arts University in the United Kingdom, she's a visual storyteller who enjoys taking a poetic approach to her art. She uses traditional painting techniques aided by digital methods.